Jazz Play-Along

Book and CD for B♭, E♭, C and Bass Clef Instruments

volume 93

Arranged and Produced by
Mark Taylor

BOOK

CD

ISBN 978-1-4234-5908-8

Disney characters and artwork © Disney Enterprises, Inc.

WALT DISNEY MUSIC COMPANY
WONDERLAND MUSIC COMPANY, INC.

DISTRIBUTED BY

HAL•LEONARD® CORPORATION

7777 W. BLUEMOUND RD. P.O. BOX 13819 MILWAUKEE, WI 53213

In Australia Contact:
Hal Leonard Australia Pty. Ltd.
4 Lentara Court
Cheltenham, Victoria, 3192 Australia
Email: ausadmin@halleonard.com.au

Visit Hal Leonard Online at
www.halleonard.com

Disney Favorites

Volume 93

Arranged and Produced by
Mark Taylor

Featured Players:

Graham Breedlove–Trumpet
Scott Silbert–Tenor Saxophone
Tony Nalker–Piano
Jim Roberts–Bass
Joe McCarthy–Drums

Recorded at Bias Studios, Springfield, Virginia
Bob Dawson, Engineer

HOW TO USE THE CD:

Each song has <u>two</u> tracks:

1) Split Track/Melody

Woodwind, Brass, Keyboard, and **Mallet Players** can use this track as a learning tool for melody style and inflection.

Bass Players can learn and perform with this track – remove the recorded bass track by turning down the volume on the LEFT channel.

Keyboard and **Guitar Players** can learn and perform with this track – remove the recorded piano part by turning down the volume on the RIGHT channel.

2) Full Stereo Track

Soloists or **Groups** can learn and perform with this accompaniment track with the RHYTHM SECTION only.

A Dream Is a Wish Your Heart Makes

FROM WALT DISNEY'S CINDERELLA

WORDS AND MUSIC BY MACK DAVID,
AL HOFFMAN AND JERRY LIVINGSTON

THE BARE NECESSITIES

FROM WALT DISNEY'S THE JUNGLE BOOK

WORDS AND MUSIC BY
TERRY GILKYSON

CD

◆ 5 : SPLIT TRACK/MELODY
◆ 6 : FULL STEREO TRACK

C VERSION

CANDLE ON THE WATER
FROM WALT DISNEY'S PETE'S DRAGON

WORDS AND MUSIC BY AL KASHA
AND JOEL HIRSCHHORN

SLOW POP ROCK

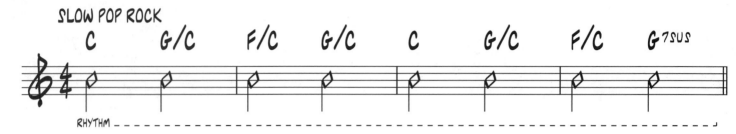

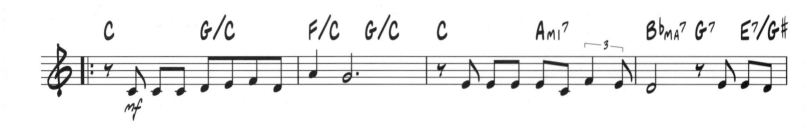

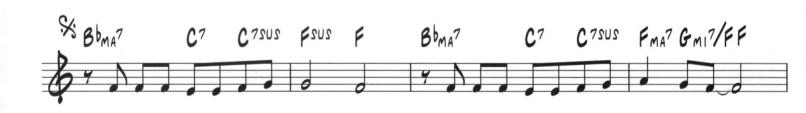

CHIM CHIM CHER-EE

FROM WALT DISNEY'S MARY POPPINS

WORDS AND MUSIC BY RICHARD M. SHERMAN
AND ROBERT B. SHERMAN

C VERSION

HE'S A TRAMP
FROM WALT DISNEY'S LADY AND THE TRAMP

WORDS AND MUSIC BY PEGGY LEE
AND SONNY BURKE

13

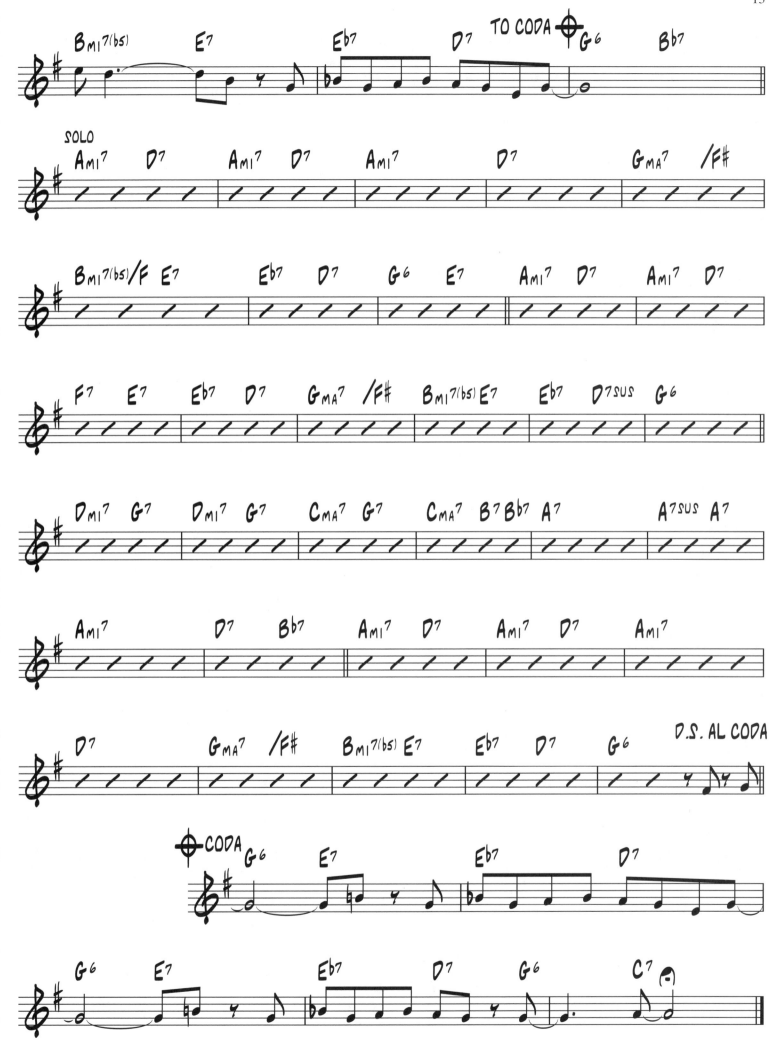

CD

C VERSION

IT'S A SMALL WORLD

FROM "IT'S A SMALL WORLD" AT DISNEYLAND PARK
AND MAGIC KINGDOM PARK

WORDS AND MUSIC BY RICHARD M. SHERMAN
AND ROBERT B. SHERMAN

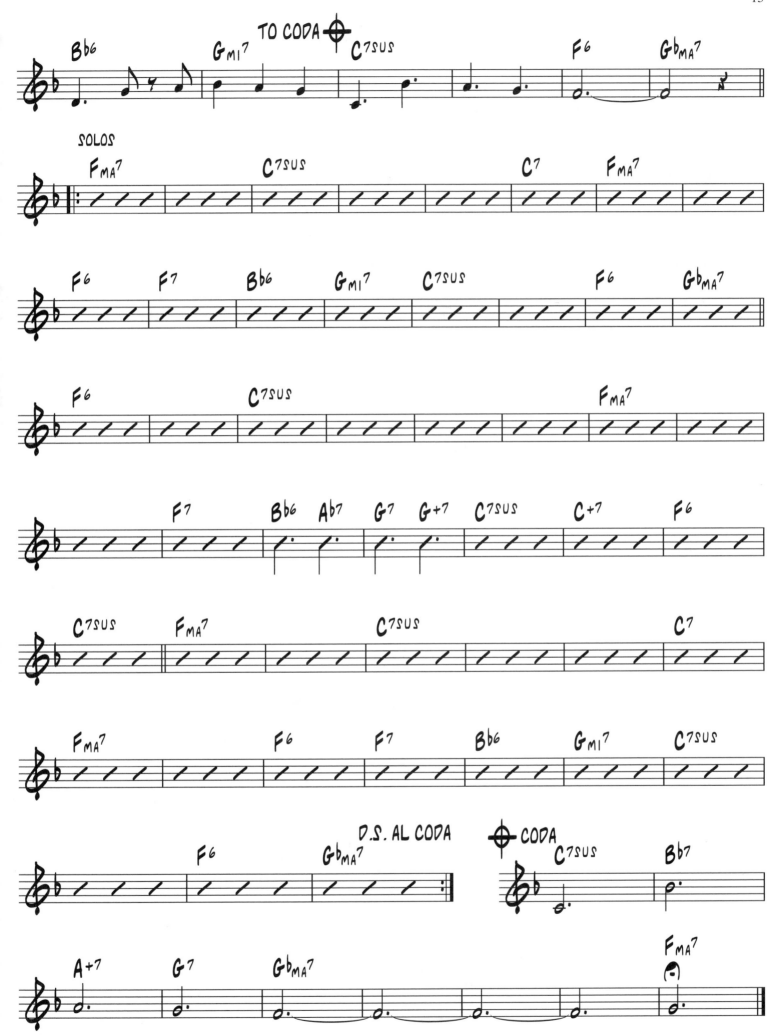

CD
13 : SPLIT TRACK/MELODY
14 : FULL STEREO TRACK

C VERSION

MICKEY MOUSE MARCH
FROM WALT DISNEY'S THE MICKEY MOUSE CLUB

WORDS AND MUSIC BY
JIMMY DODD

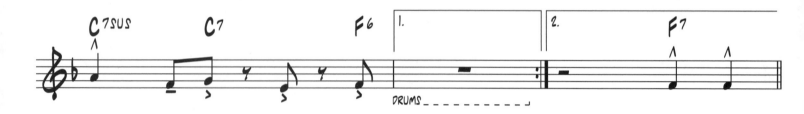

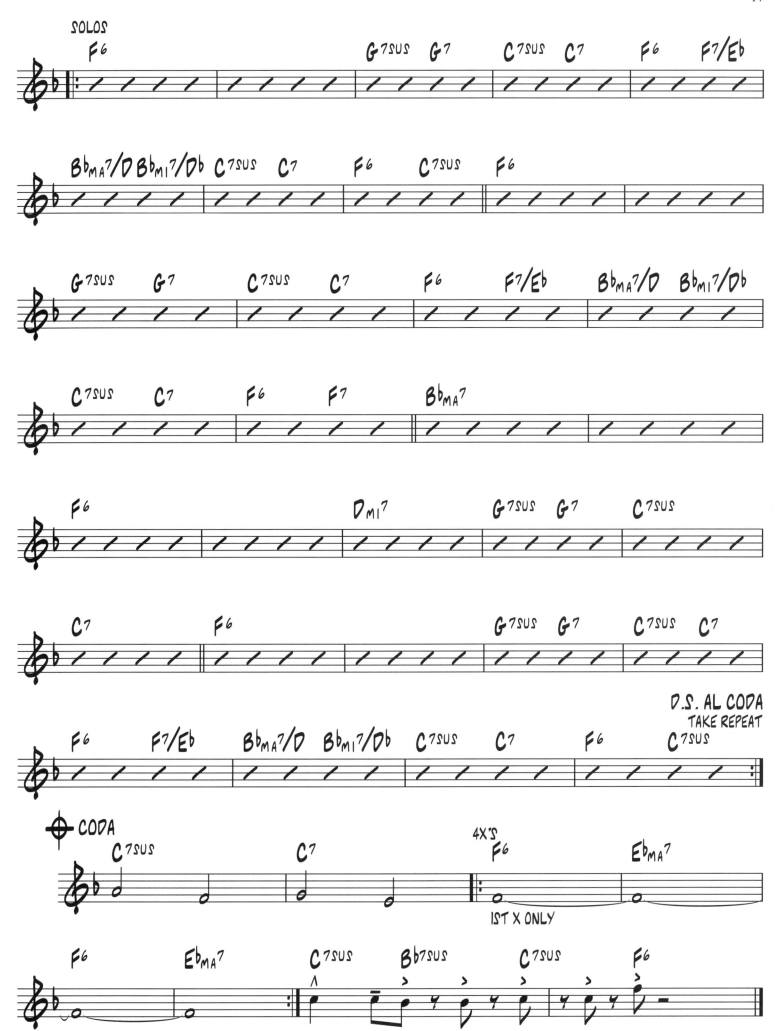

ONCE UPON A DREAM
FROM WALT DISNEY'S SLEEPING BEAUTY

WORDS AND MUSIC BY SAMMY FAIN
AND JACK LAWRENCE
ADAPTED FROM A THEME BY TCHAIKOVSKY

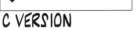

C VERSION

UNDER THE SEA
FROM WALT DISNEY'S THE LITTLE MERMAID

MUSIC BY ALAN MENKEN
LYRICS BY HOWARD ASHMAN

CD
🔷 17 : SPLIT TRACK/MELODY
🔷 18 : FULL STEREO TRACK

C VERSION

22

A WHOLE NEW WORLD
FROM WALT DISNEY'S ALADDIN

MUSIC BY ALAN MENKEN
LYRICS BY TIM RICE

C VERSION

A DREAM IS A WISH
YOUR HEART MAKES

FROM WALT DISNEY'S CINDERELLA

WORDS AND MUSIC BY MACK DAVID,
AL HOFFMAN AND JERRY LIVINGSTON

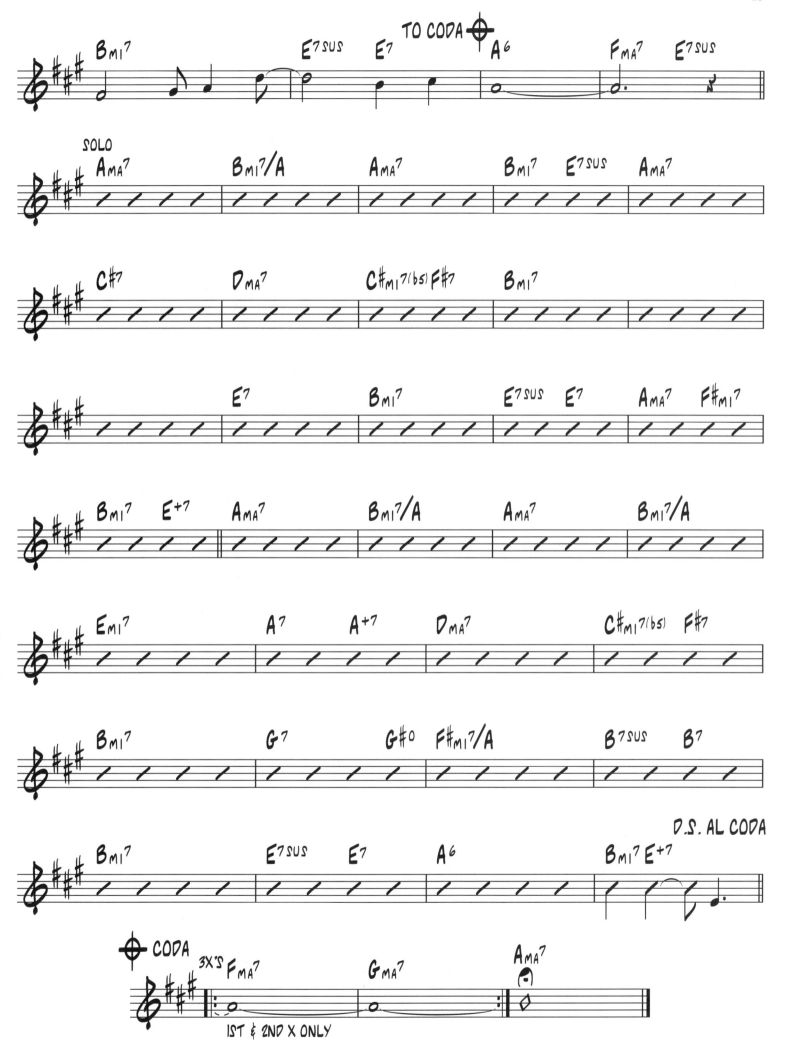

CD
◆ 3 : SPLIT TRACK/MELODY
◆ 4 : FULL STEREO TRACK

Bb VERSION

THE BARE NECESSITIES
FROM WALT DISNEY'S THE JUNGLE BOOK

WORDS AND MUSIC BY
TERRY GILKYSON

CANDLE ON THE WATER

FROM WALT DISNEY'S PETE'S DRAGON

WORDS AND MUSIC BY AL KASHA
AND JOEL HIRSCHHORN

Bb VERSION

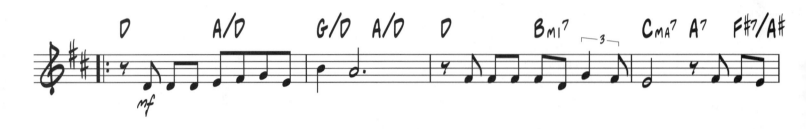

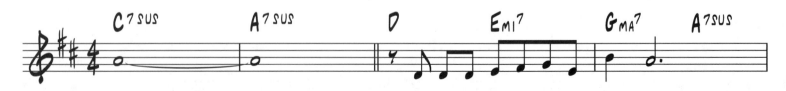

CD
◆ **7** : SPLIT TRACK/MELODY
◆ **8** : FULL STEREO TRACK

Bb VERSION

CHIM CHIM CHER-EE

FROM WALT DISNEY'S MARY POPPINS

WORDS AND MUSIC BY RICHARD M. SHERMAN
AND ROBERT B. SHERMAN

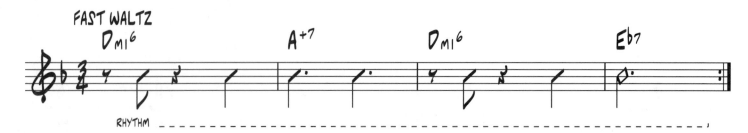

HE'S A TRAMP
FROM WALT DISNEY'S LADY AND THE TRAMP

WORDS AND MUSIC BY PEGGY LEE
AND SONNY BURKE

Bb VERSION

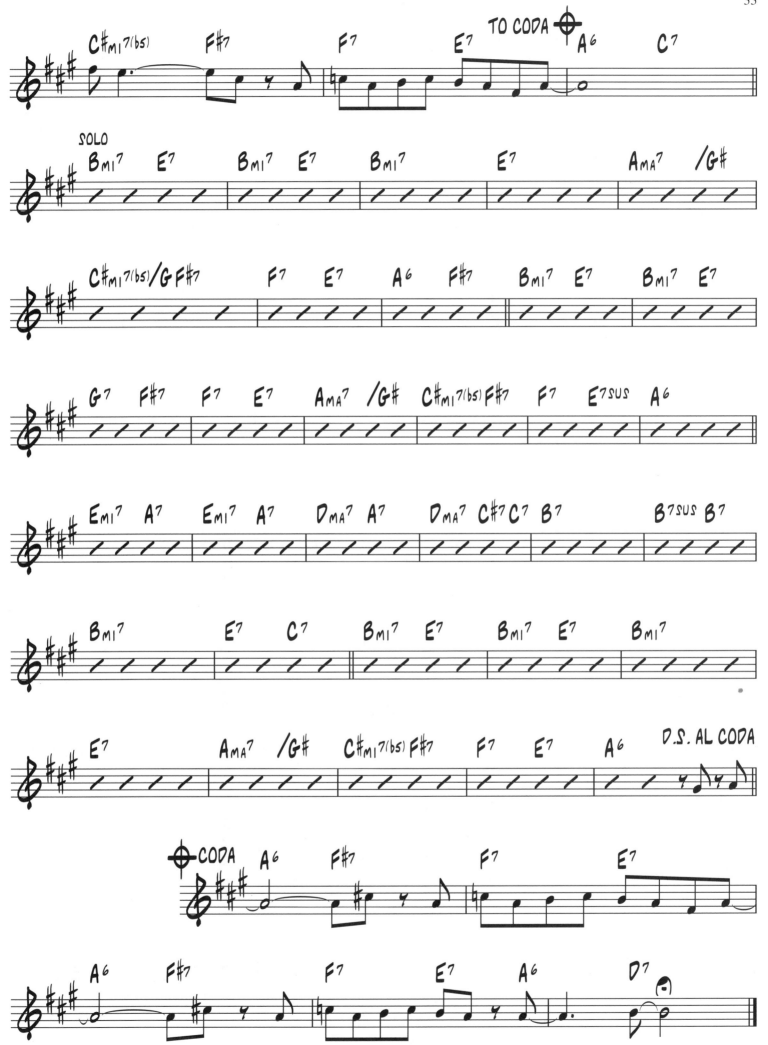

IT'S A SMALL WORLD

FROM "IT'S A SMALL WORLD" AT DISNEYLAND PARK
AND MAGIC KINGDOM PARK

WORDS AND MUSIC BY RICHARD M. SHERMAN
AND ROBERT B. SHERMAN

CD
11: SPLIT TRACK/MELODY
12: FULL STEREO TRACK

Bb VERSION

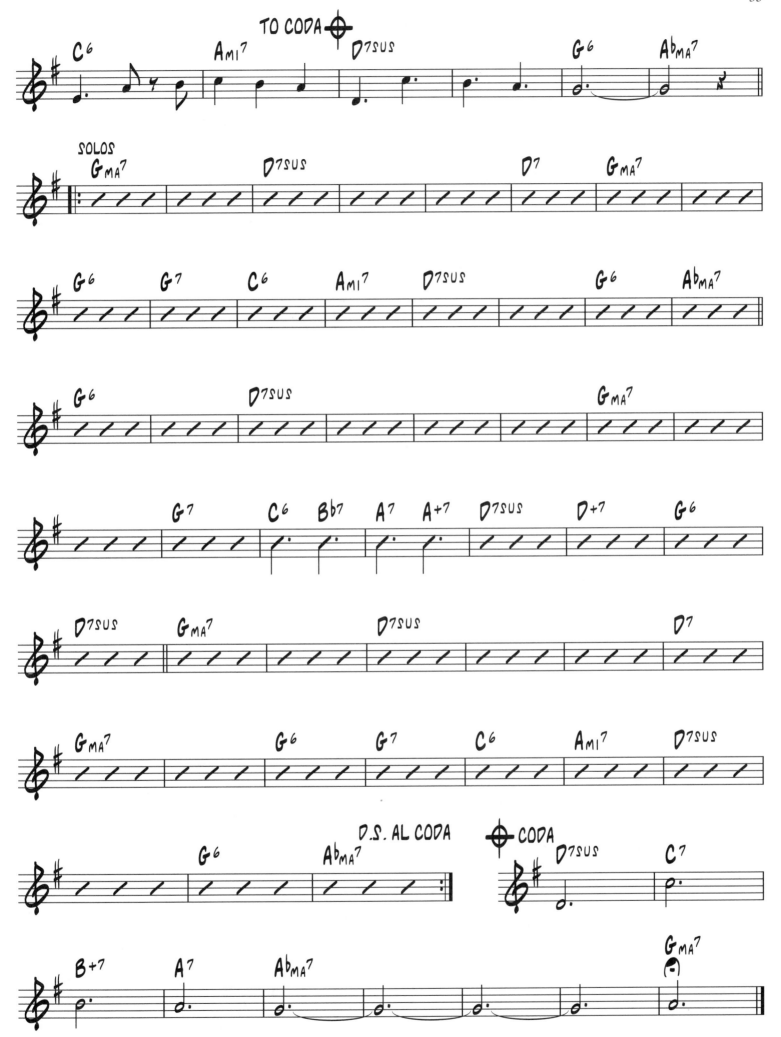

CD
13 : SPLIT TRACK/MELODY
14 : FULL STEREO TRACK

MICKEY MOUSE MARCH
FROM WALT DISNEY'S THE MICKEY MOUSE CLUB

WORDS AND MUSIC BY
JIMMY DODD

Bb VERSION

ONCE UPON A DREAM
FROM WALT DISNEY'S SLEEPING BEAUTY

WORDS AND MUSIC BY SAMMY FAIN
AND JACK LAWRENCE
ADAPTED FROM A THEME BY TCHAIKOVSKY

CD
- 🔷**15** : SPLIT TRACK/MELODY
- 🔷**16** : FULL STEREO TRACK

Bb VERSION

UNDER THE SEA
FROM WALT DISNEY'S THE LITTLE MERMAID

MUSIC BY ALAN MENKEN
LYRICS BY HOWARD ASHMAN

Bb VERSION

A WHOLE NEW WORLD
FROM WALT DISNEY'S ALADDIN

MUSIC BY ALAN MENKEN
LYRICS BY TIM RICE

Bb VERSION

43

CD

1 : SPLIT TRACK/MELODY
2 : FULL STEREO TRACK

Eb VERSION

A DREAM IS A WISH
YOUR HEART MAKES

FROM WALT DISNEY'S CINDERELLA

WORDS AND MUSIC BY MACK DAVID,
AL HOFFMAN AND JERRY LIVINGSTON

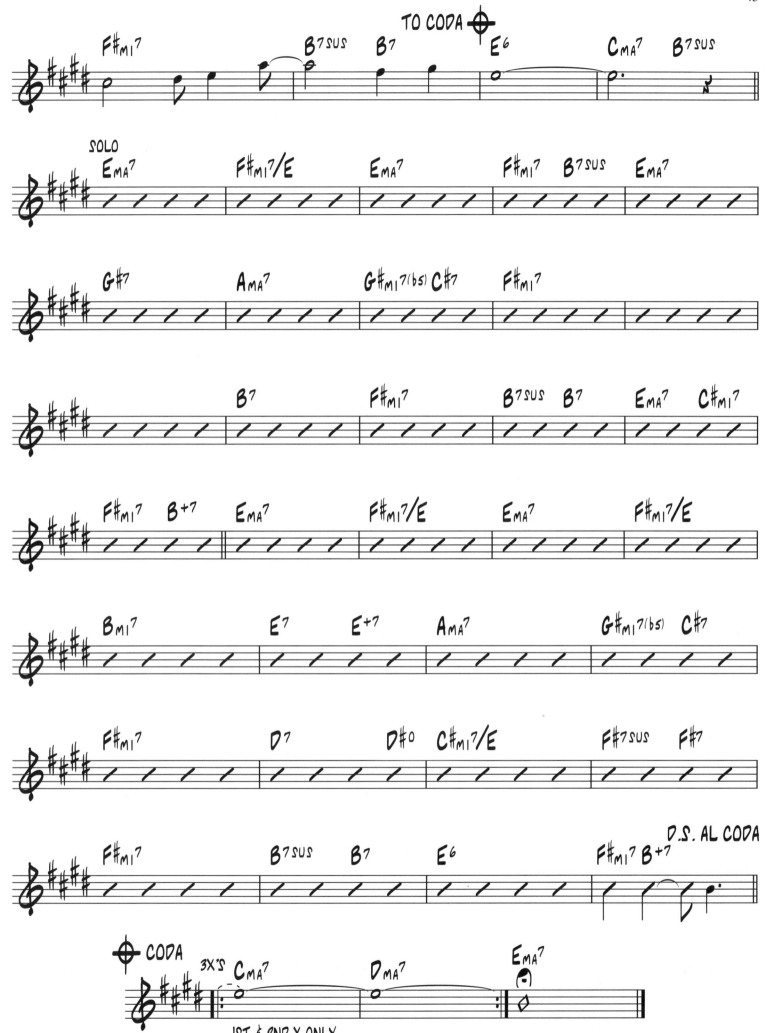

CD

3 : SPLIT TRACK/MELODY
4 : FULL STEREO TRACK

THE BARE NECESSITIES
FROM WALT DISNEY'S THE JUNGLE BOOK

WORDS AND MUSIC BY
TERRY GILKYSON

Eb VERSION

CANDLE ON THE WATER

FROM WALT DISNEY'S PETE'S DRAGON

WORDS AND MUSIC BY AL KASHA
AND JOEL HIRSCHHORN

Eb VERSION

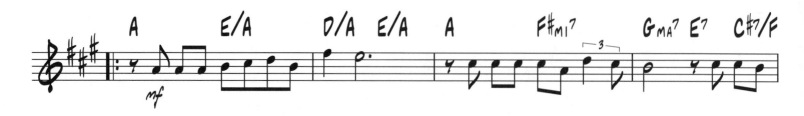

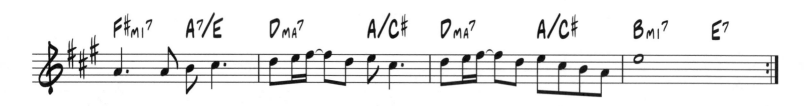

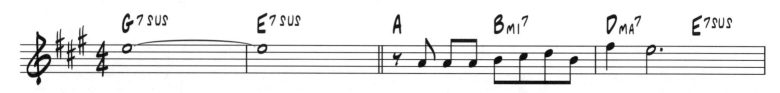

CD

7 : SPLIT TRACK/MELODY
8 : FULL STEREO TRACK

Eb VERSION

CHIM CHIM CHER–EE

FROM WALT DISNEY'S MARY POPPINS

WORDS AND MUSIC BY RICHARD M. SHERMAN
AND ROBERT B. SHERMAN

HE'S A TRAMP
FROM WALT DISNEY'S LADY AND THE TRAMP

WORDS AND MUSIC BY PEGGY LEE
AND SONNY BURKE

CD
◆ 9 : SPLIT TRACK/MELODY
◆ 10 : FULL STEREO TRACK

Eb VERSION

CD

⑪ : SPLIT TRACK/MELODY
⑫ : FULL STEREO TRACK

IT'S A SMALL WORLD

FROM "IT'S A SMALL WORLD" AT DISNEYLAND PARK
AND MAGIC KINGDOM PARK

WORDS AND MUSIC BY RICHARD M. SHERMAN
AND ROBERT B. SHERMAN

Eb VERSION

MICKEY MOUSE MARCH
FROM WALT DISNEY'S THE MICKEY MOUSE CLUB

CD
13 : SPLIT TRACK/MELODY
14 : FULL STEREO TRACK

Eb VERSION

WORDS AND MUSIC BY
JIMMY DODD

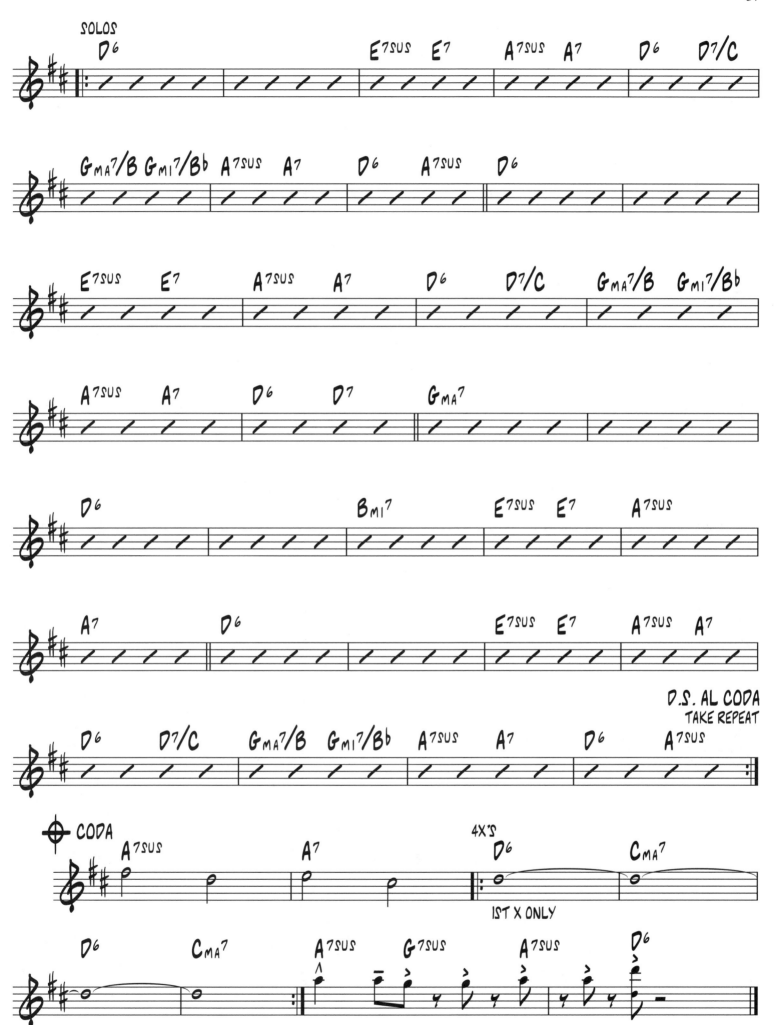

CD
15 : SPLIT TRACK/MELODY
16 : FULL STEREO TRACK

Eb VERSION

ONCE UPON A DREAM
FROM WALT DISNEY'S SLEEPING BEAUTY

WORDS AND MUSIC BY SAMMY FAIN
AND JACK LAWRENCE
ADAPTED FROM A THEME BY TCHAIKOVSKY

UNDER THE SEA
FROM WALT DISNEY'S THE LITTLE MERMAID

MUSIC BY ALAN MENKEN
LYRICS BY HOWARD ASHMAN

Eb VERSION

A WHOLE NEW WORLD

FROM WALT DISNEY'S ALADDIN

MUSIC BY ALAN MENKEN
LYRICS BY TIM RICE

Eb VERSION

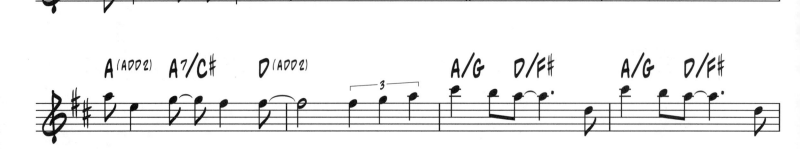

CD
1 : SPLIT TRACK/MELODY
2 : FULL STEREO TRACK

A DREAM IS A WISH
YOUR HEART MAKES

FROM WALT DISNEY'S CINDERELLA

WORDS AND MUSIC BY MACK DAVID,
AL HOFFMAN AND JERRY LIVINGSTON

𝄢: C VERSION

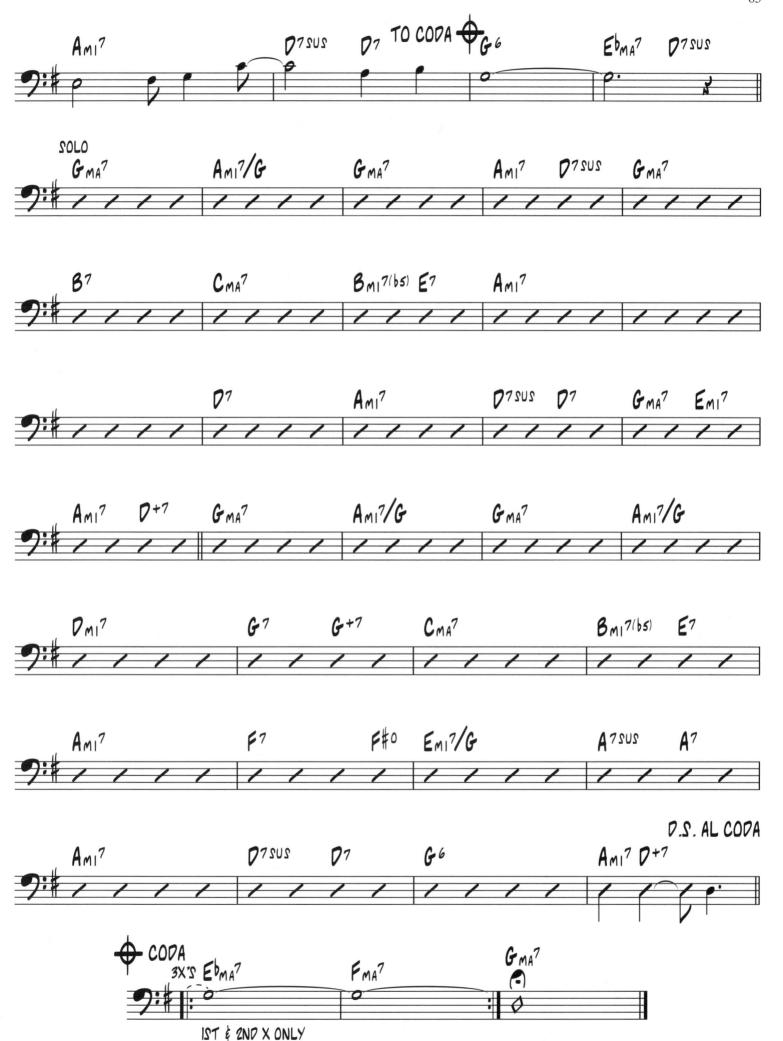

THE BARE NECESSITIES
FROM WALT DISNEY'S THE JUNGLE BOOK

WORDS AND MUSIC BY
TERRY GILKYSON

CD

⑤ : SPLIT TRACK/MELODY
⑥ : FULL STEREO TRACK

𝄢: C VERSION

Candle on the Water

FROM WALT DISNEY'S PETE'S DRAGON

WORDS AND MUSIC BY AL KASHA
AND JOEL HIRSCHHORN

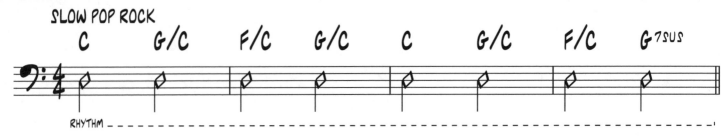

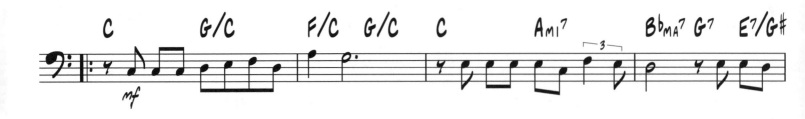

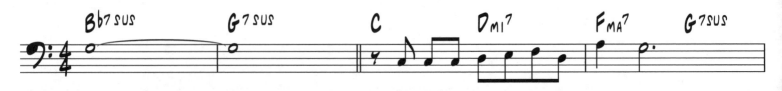

CD

◆ **7** : SPLIT TRACK/MELODY
◆ **8** : FULL STEREO TRACK

𝄢 : C VERSION

CHIM CHIM CHER-EE

FROM WALT DISNEY'S MARY POPPINS

WORDS AND MUSIC BY RICHARD M. SHERMAN
AND ROBERT B. SHERMAN

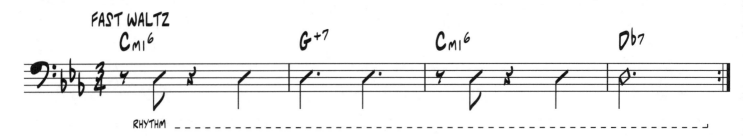

HE'S A TRAMP
FROM WALT DISNEY'S LADY AND THE TRAMP

WORDS AND MUSIC BY PEGGY LEE
AND SONNY BURKE

IT'S A SMALL WORLD

FROM "IT'S A SMALL WORLD" AT DISNEYLAND PARK
AND MAGIC KINGDOM PARK

WORDS AND MUSIC BY RICHARD M. SHERMAN
AND ROBERT B. SHERMAN

CD
- **11**: SPLIT TRACK/MELODY
- **12**: FULL STEREO TRACK

𝄢: C VERSION

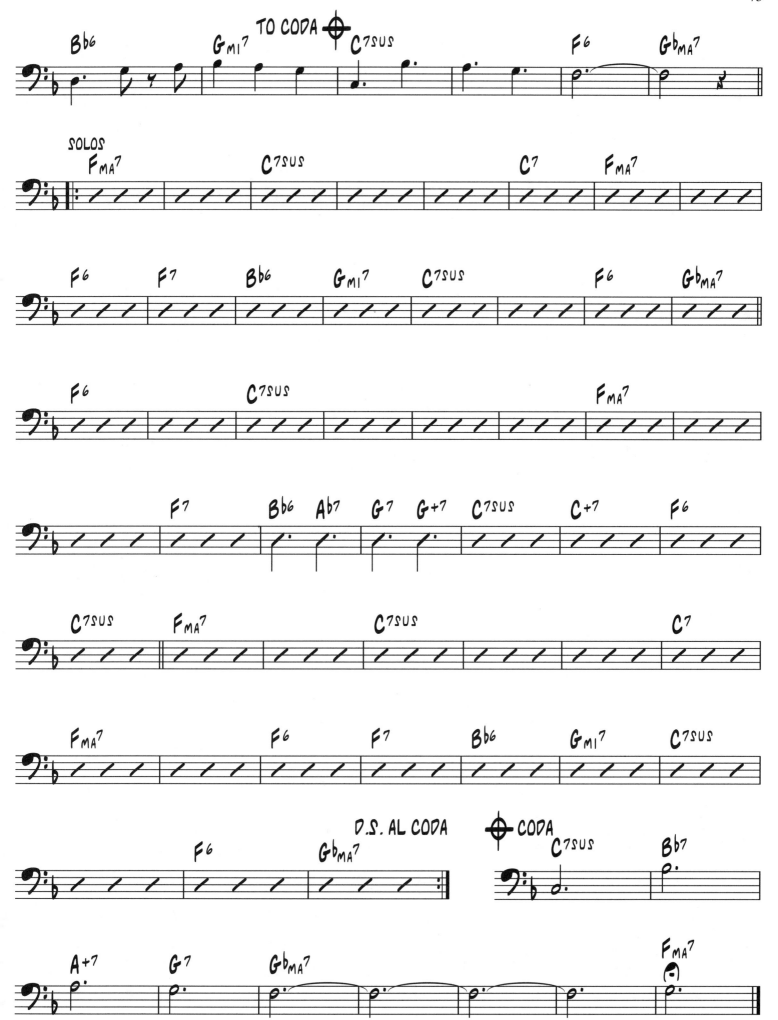

CD
- **13** : SPLIT TRACK/MELODY
- **14** : FULL STEREO TRACK

MICKEY MOUSE MARCH
FROM WALT DISNEY'S THE MICKEY MOUSE CLUB

WORDS AND MUSIC BY
JIMMY DODD

C VERSION

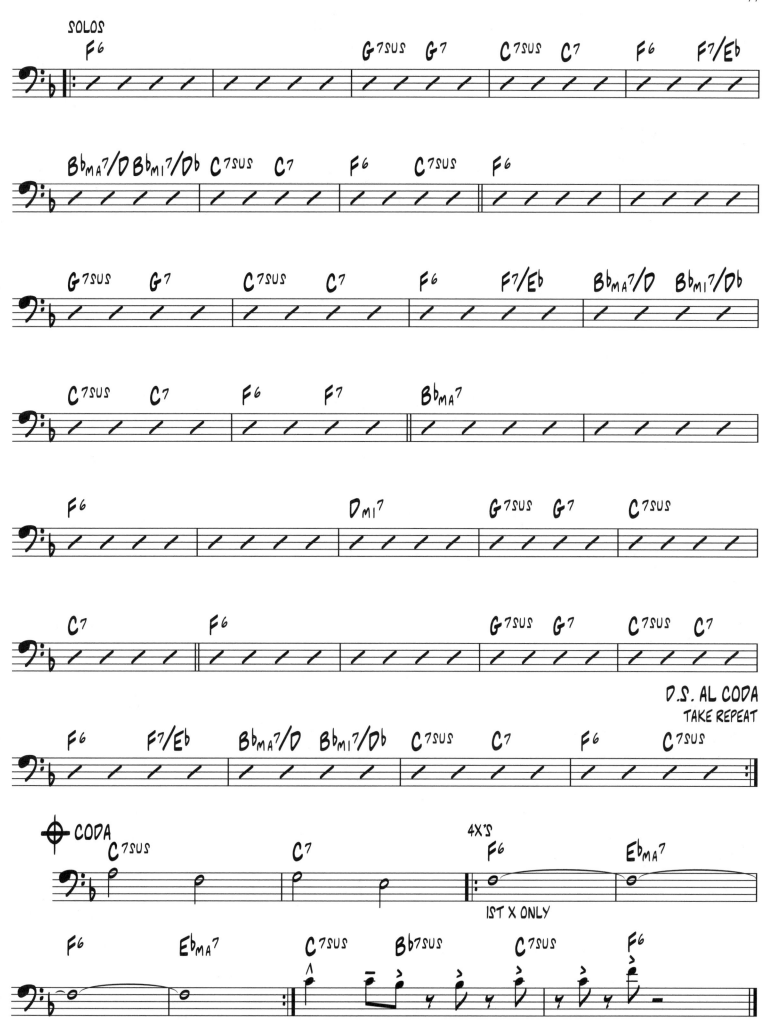

ONCE UPON A DREAM
FROM WALT DISNEY'S SLEEPING BEAUTY

WORDS AND MUSIC BY SAMMY FAIN
AND JACK LAWRENCE
ADAPTED FROM A THEME BY TCHAIKOVSKY

UNDER THE SEA
FROM WALT DISNEY'S THE LITTLE MERMAID

MUSIC BY ALAN MENKEN
LYRICS BY HOWARD ASHMAN

A WHOLE NEW WORLD
FROM WALT DISNEY'S ALADDIN

MUSIC BY ALAN MENKEN
LYRICS BY TIM RICE

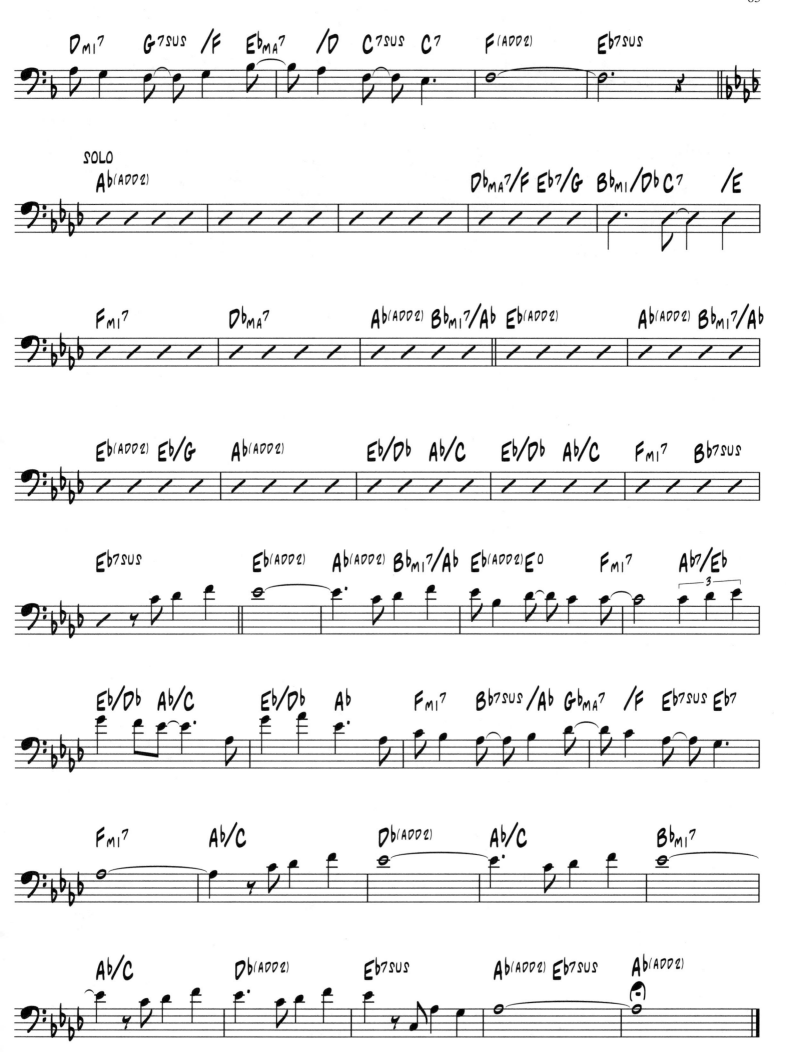